GAME ON!

MARIO

PAIGE V. POLINSKY

**Checkerboard
Library**

An Imprint of Abdo Publishing
abdobooks.com

abdobooks.com

Published by Abdo Publishing, a division of ABDO, PO Box 398166, Minneapolis, Minnesota 55439.
Copyright © 2020 by Abdo Consulting Group, Inc. International copyrights reserved in all countries.
No part of this book may be reproduced in any form without written permission from the publisher.
Checkerboard Library™ is a trademark and logo of Abdo Publishing.

Printed in the United States of America, North Mankato, Minnesota
102019
012020

THIS BOOK CONTAINS
RECYCLED MATERIALS

Design: Aruna Rangarajan, Mighty Media, Inc.
Production: Mighty Media, Inc.
Editor: Megan Borgert-Spaniol
Design Elements: Shutterstock Images
Cover Photograph: Pexels
Interior Photographs: Antoine Turmel/Flickr, p. 25 (top); BagoGames/Flickr, pp. 18, 23, 29 (right);
Casey Curry/AP Images, p. 7; Daniel Costa/Flickr, p. 11; giochi/Flickr, pp. 12, 13; Jeff Egnaczyk/Flickr,
pp. 24, 28; Matthew Paul Argall/Flickr, p. 28 (top left); mattjerome_88/Flickr, p. 21; nOcturbulous/
Flickr, p. 29; Pexels, p. 28 (bottom left); Rob Boudon/Flickr, p. 9; Shutterstock Images, pp. 5, 15, 17, 25
(bottom), 27, 28 (bottom right)

Library of Congress Control Number: 2019943320

Publisher's Cataloging-in-Publication Data
Names: Polinsky, Paige V., author.
Title: Mario / by Paige V. Polinsky
Description: Minneapolis, Minnesota : Abdo Publishing, 2020 | Series: Game on! | Includes online
    resources and index.
Identifiers: ISBN 9781532191671 (lib. bdg.) | ISBN 9781644942826 (pbk.) | ISBN 9781532178405 (ebook)
Subjects: LCSH: Video games--Juvenile literature. | Super Mario Bros. (Game)--Juvenile literature. |
    Nintendo video games--Juvenile literature. | Video game characters--Juvenile literature. | Video
    games and children--Juvenile literature.
Classification: DDC 794.8--dc23

NOTE TO READERS

Video games that depict shooting or other violent acts should be subject to adult discretion and
awareness that exposure to such acts may affect players' perceptions of violence in the real world.

CONTENTS

MUSHROOM KINGDOM

A short, jolly man leaps through grassy hills. He dives into a well and pops out of a green pipe. The man hops across floating bricks in search of coins and shimmering stars. Go, Mario, go!

Mario is a friendly little plumber who stars in the world's best-selling video game **franchise**. Nintendo's *Mario* features more than 180 different titles, including the famous *Super Mario* series. In these **platformers**, Mario travels through the magical Mushroom Kingdom with his brother, Luigi. They must rescue Princess Peach from the evil King Bowser. Along the way, they fight enemies and collect coins.

Nintendo has sold more than 555 million *Mario* games. The plumber stars in sports titles, party minigames, and **role-playing games (RPGs)**. *Mario Kart* racing games

MUSTACHED MAN

Mario's mustache makes him look quite mature. But according to creator Shigeru Miyamoto, he is only 24 or 25 years old!

Mario characters have been made into countless toy products. In 2014, Nintendo promoted the new *Mario Kart 8* with a set of McDonald's Happy Meal toys!

are a fan favorite, and *Super Mario* is still going strong. Its 2017 title, *Super Mario Odyssey*, sold more than 14 million copies. The *Mario* **franchise** is famous around the world!

NINTENDO'S ARTIST

Mario's creator, Shigeru Miyamoto, was born in Japan in 1952. As a child, Miyamoto loved to explore hills and caves. Young Miyamoto also loved drawing and painting. He drew cartoons and dreamed of becoming a comic book artist.

In 1970, Miyamoto began school at Japan's Kanazawa College of Art. He studied **industrial design**. After graduating in 1975, Miyamoto sought a job at toy company Nintendo. He was hired as the company's first staff artist!

At the time, Nintendo was new to the video game industry. The company hoped to break into North America's **arcade** market. In 1979, Nintendo's Minoru Arakawa opened a US office in New York City. He ordered 3,000 copies of Nintendo's *Radar Scope* shooter game to sell in the US.

Radar Scope was popular in Japan. But US gamers were not impressed. Only 1,000 copies sold. To bounce back, Nintendo needed a fresh arcade title. It was Miyamoto's time to shine!

Miyamoto is also famous for creating the popular video game *The Legend of Zelda.*

JUMPING TO STARDOM

Miyamoto and engineer Gunpei Yokoi created the first true **platformer**. It featured a carpenter and his pet gorilla, Donkey Kong. Kong kidnaps the carpenter's girlfriend. Players had to jump across platforms and dodge attacks to save her.

Miyamoto designed *Donkey Kong*'s carpenter to be a silly, everyday guy. He was short and round with a mustache, big nose, and red overalls. Workers at Nintendo's Washington warehouse thought the carpenter looked like their building's landlord, Mario Segale. They began calling the character "Mario." Miyamoto was an instant fan of the name!

Donkey Kong launched in July 1981. No other video game at the time let players jump! **Arcades** went crazy for *Donkey Kong*. By 1982, Nintendo had earned $180 million from the game. It was the fastest-selling video game ever.

Mario starred in two more *Donkey Kong* games before getting a title of his own. In July 1983, *Mario Bros.* **debuted**.

The maze-filled *Ms. Pac-Man* game came out the same year as *Donkey Kong*. These two games were among the greatest hits of the 1980s and are considered arcade classics.

The two-player **platformer** featured Mario as a plumber in the sewers of New York City. It also introduced Mario's brother, Luigi. *Mario Bros.* was the start of something huge!

SUPER SIDE-SCROLLERS

In August 1983, Nintendo wowed Japan with a new **console**. The Family Computer (Famicom) was the perfect device for a bigger, better *Mario*. Miyamoto's team designed new land, sea, and sky stages for *Super Mario Bros.* While most games had fixed screens, this **platformer** was a **side-scroller**. It let players travel through worlds from left to right.

Super Mario Bros. was released in Japan in September 1985. It introduced key characters, like Bowser and Princess Peach. Their bright, dreamy Mushroom Kingdom charmed gamers. In October, *Super Mario Bros.* hit North America. Nintendo bundled it with a remodeled Famicom console called the Nintendo Entertainment System (NES). *Super Mario Bros.* became history's best-selling video game!

In June 1986, *Super Mario Bros. 2* dropped in Japan. This single-player platformer was popular but extremely difficult. Nintendo worried it would put off North American players.

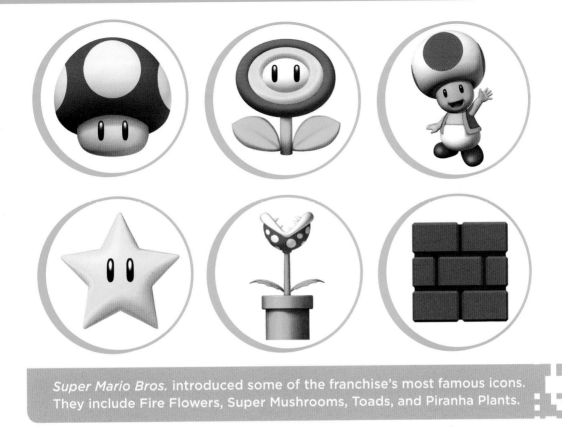

Super Mario Bros. introduced some of the franchise's most famous icons. They include Fire Flowers, Super Mushrooms, Toads, and Piranha Plants.

So, North America received an easier *Super Mario Bros. 2* in October 1988. The gameplay felt different from the first *Super Mario Bros.* Instead of stomping on enemies, players picked them up and threw them. But *Mario* fans loved it all the same.

In February 1990, *Super Mario Bros. 3* hit North America. It featured fresh items, moves, and enemies. All 250,000 copies sold out within 48 hours. Gamers had *Mario* mania!

TRACK COMPOSERS

Mario features some of the most well-known music in video game history. Nintendo's talented composers write each song. The music must be catchy, creative, and memorable. Most importantly, it must match whatever is happening in the game.

Koji Kondo wrote many of *Mario*'s most popular tunes. "I aim for music that is happy," he says. Kondo's *Super Mario Bros.* music starred bongos, steel drums, and other instruments. Its bright, rhythmic feel guides *Mario* music to this day.

Nintendo's composers use early in-game images to begin brainstorming new music. Eventually, they get models of the game to play. They often create songs directly on computers using special programs. Sometimes they arrange music to be performed by live musicians.

Each *Mario* title brings new challenges for composers. But the hard work is worth it. When Kondo gets a song just right, he listens to it again and again. "I'll even dance to it!"

SUPER MARIO BROS.

THE SOUND OF SUCCESS

At first, Kondo wrote a relaxed, light melody for the main track of *Super Mario Bros.* But when he played it back alongside the game, the speed and rhythm were off. After some experimenting, Kondo came up with a 'cha-cha-cha' melody. Today, that melody is one of the most famous video game tracks of all time!

MARIO MAGIC

Mario was on a roll. However, Nintendo fell behind as other companies launched new **consoles**. To catch up, it created the Super Famicom, a console with improved **graphics** and sound. Meanwhile, Nintendo designed the biggest, brightest *Mario* game yet. *Super Mario World* featured more than 70 levels and a new major character, Yoshi the dinosaur.

In August 1991, the Super Famicom launched in North America as the Super Nintendo Entertainment System (SNES). It included *Super Mario World* for free. The SNES was a smash hit. More than 2.2 million consoles sold by December!

More SNES surprises were on the way. Miyamoto's team was creating a two-player racing game with split-screen play. A few months in, developers placed Mario in a kart for fun. Everyone loved it! So, developers gave the entire game a *Mario* twist.

Super Mario Kart dropped in August 1992. It featured quick, colorful courses and classic racing modes, such as Grand Prix.

In 1989, *Super Mario Land* debuted on Nintendo's new handheld Game Boy console. Later, the upgraded Game Boy Color also supported the game.

Super Mario Kart was a whole new take on Mushroom Kingdom, and it quickly became a fan favorite.

NOW IN 3-D!

In 1996, *Mario* reached incredible new heights. *Super Mario RPG: Legend of the Seven Stars* **debuted** that March. In it, Mario and friends must work together to collect seven stars and defeat the evil Smithy Gang. Critics praised its strong **graphics** and funny writing. But a bigger, better game would soon steal the show. Miyamoto was creating a launch title for Nintendo's new **console**, the Nintendo 64 (N64). It would be the first *Mario* **platformer** with fully **3-D** graphics!

Super Mario 64 (SM64) would let gamers explore Mario's world in greater detail than ever. Most 3-D games at the time presented the action through a character's eyes or from a fixed point. But in *SM64*, players could control the view. They could change the angle or zoom in and out whenever they wanted. This dynamic viewing system was among the first of its kind.

Nintendo launched *SM64* and the N64 in June 1996. *SM64*'s graphics amazed gamers everywhere. Its levels were fun and

Super Mario 64 is the best-selling Nintendo 64 game of all time.

exciting to explore. The video game sold nearly 12 million copies and set the standard for all **3-D platformers**.

In December 1996, Mario returned to the track in *Mario Kart 64*. It was the first four-player *Mario* game. Fans loved racing friends through 3-D courses filled with ramps, hills, and curves.

Nintendo went on to make several sequels to *Paper Mario*. *Paper Mario: Color Splash* was released for the Wii U console in 2016.

In 1998, Nintendo launched a series that made four-player gaming more popular than ever. *Mario Party* **debuted** in December. This digital board game offered a totally new *Mario* experience. Players traveled the board and competed in wacky minigames to gather coins and stars. In one game, players dove for sunken treasure. In another, they skipped over a flaming jump rope!

Meanwhile, Nintendo created a *Mario* **RPG** for gamers with less experience. *Mario Story* was packed with puzzles and battles. Players adventured with **2-D** characters through **3-D** settings. In February 2001, the game hit North America as *Paper Mario*. Some critics complained it was too easy. But far more people fell in love with the game.

That September, Nintendo released its new GameCube **console**. The GameCube did not feature a new *Mario* **platformer**. However, directors Yoshiaki Koizumi and Kenta Usui were working hard to change that.

SUNSHINE & OUTER SPACE

Koizumi and Usui were creating a *Super Mario 64* **sequel** for the GameCube. The **3-D platformer** *Super Mario Sunshine* took place at a tropical resort. The game introduced Mario's new **jetpack**, which could spray objects and enemies with water!

Sunshine arrived in North America in August 2002. Its bright **graphics**, clever puzzles, and new features stunned critics. Some called it the best *Mario* yet!

Sunshine's directors wanted to create a game featuring **spherical** worlds. In 2004, they began developing a *Mario* platformer set in space. Nintendo launched *Super Mario Galaxy* in November 2007 with the Wii. This wireless **console** featured motion-capture gameplay.

Galaxy used the Wii's controllers to navigate Mario through thrilling missions and fights. Spherical stages and changing gravity levels gave the platformer a challenging twist. By 2008, *Galaxy* had won several different "Game of the Year" awards!

SUPER MARIO GALAXY 2

Super Mario Galaxy 2 came out in 2010 with new levels, twists, and secrets to discover. Players were blown away by the sequel's fresh and exciting take on the original.

MORE & MORE *MARIO*

In November 2012, Nintendo launched the Wii U. Players enjoyed its **2-D side-scroller**, *New Super Mario Bros. U*. But the **console** struggled. Its tablet controller was confusing, and there were few titles available. Nintendo tried to spark more interest with *Super Mario 3D World* in 2013. The four-player **platformer** amazed gamers with its **graphics**, music, and level design.

In May 2014, Nintendo released *Mario Kart 8* (*MK8*) on the Wii U. The 12-player title featured **high-definition** graphics. *MK8* became the best-selling Wii U game.

In September 2015, Nintendo launched a Wii U game unlike any other. In *Super Mario Maker*, players could design the *Mario* platformer of their dreams! *Maker* included tools for gamers to create their own stages. Players could share completed work online. They could play and rank other users' creations too.

Games like *Maker* offered fresh ways to enjoy *Mario*. Meanwhile, new twists on classic favorites kept fans hooked.

Mario Kart 8 introduced antigravity zones that let players race upside down!

In October 2017, Nintendo released the latest *Super Mario* title on its new Switch **console**. *Super Mario Odyssey*'s open-ended adventures let players explore more than ever before. In its first two months, the game sold more than 9 million copies!

LEVEL UP!

Mario Kart: Super to Deluxe

In April 2017, Nintendo launched *MK8* on the Switch as *Mario Kart 8 Deluxe*. On its launch day alone, it sold more than 459,000 copies in the US. By March 2019, it was the best-selling Switch title!

1992

SUPER MARIO KART

+ **Console**: SNES

+ Players: 1 or 2

+ 8 playable characters

+ 20 tracks

+ 9 items, including Banana Peel (causes other racers to spin out) and Lightning Bolt (causes other racers to move slower)

+ Modes: Mario Kart Grand Prix, Time Trial, Match Race, Battle

MARIO KART 8 DELUXE

+ **Console**: Switch

+ Players: 1 to 12

+ 42 playable characters

+ 48 tracks

+ 23 items, including Boo (a ghost that lets users pass through items and steal from opponents) and Feather (launches user's kart into the air to avoid obstacles)

+ Modes: Grand Prix, Time Trials, VS Race, Battle

Switch handheld console

COMING TO LIFE

Gamers love *Mario*, and the future of the **franchise** looks bright. In May 2019, *Super Mario Kart* entered the World Video Game Hall of Fame. That same month, Nintendo launched an invite-only early version of *Mario Kart Tour*. The **mobile** game featured racetracks from the entire *Mario Kart* series.

Super Mario Maker 2 dropped on the Switch in June 2019. In its new multiplayer mode, up to four players could race through player-made creations. The game also featured a story mode as well as new tools, course parts, and premade levels.

Mushroom Kingdom is coming to life in bigger ways, too. In 2020, Nintendo and Universal Studios will open a theme park in Japan called Super Nintendo World. The park will feature *Mario*-themed rides, shops, and restaurants! A *Super Mario Bros*. movie is also set for release in 2022.

For more than 35 years, players have jumped, raced, and partied their way through Mushroom Kingdom. Why?

Tour companies in Tokyo, Japan, let visitors live out their *Mario Kart* dreams. Tourists suit up in *Mario*-themed costumes and zoom around the city streets!

Miyamoto believes it is because *Mario* lets gamers play in fun, creative ways. "That's the key to what has made *Mario* so accepted and popular," he says. Miyamoto's roly-poly plumber will always be a shining star!

TIMELINE

1981

Mario first appears in *Donkey Kong*.

1985

Super Mario Bros. is released in Japan.

1992

Super Mario Kart drops in August.

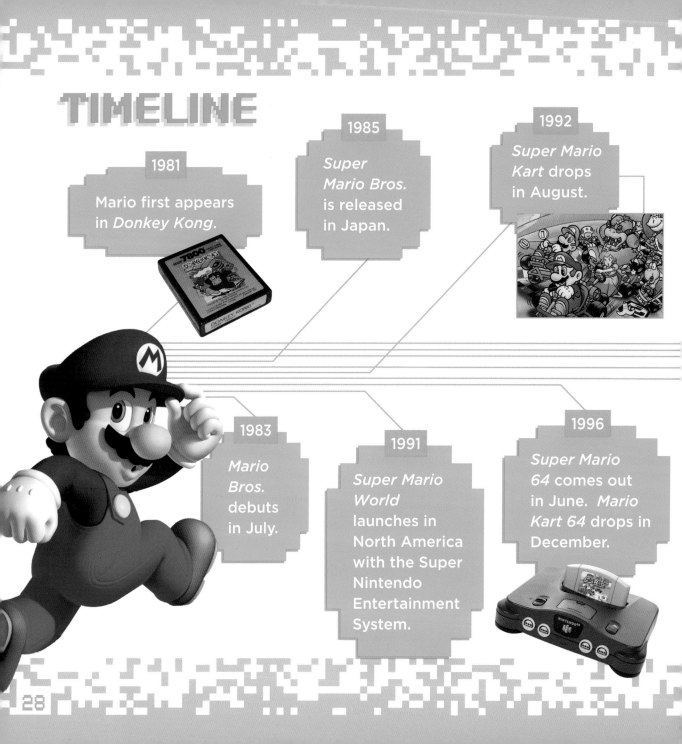

1983

Mario Bros. debuts in July.

1991

Super Mario World launches in North America with the Super Nintendo Entertainment System.

1996

Super Mario 64 comes out in June. *Mario Kart 64* drops in December.

2007

Super Mario Galaxy is released for the Nintendo Wii.

2015

Super Mario Maker launches for the Wii U.

2014

Nintendo releases *Mario Kart 8* for the Wii U.

2017

Mario Kart 8 Deluxe launches on the Nintendo Switch in April. *Super Mario Odyssey* arrives in October.

GLOSSARY

arcade—a business in which electronic game machines, such as pinball, can be played for entertainment.

console—an electronic system used to play video games.

debut (DAY-byoo)—to first appear.

franchise—a series of related works, such as movies or video games, that feature the same characters.

graphics—images on the screen of a computer, TV, or other device.

high-definition—having a high degree of detail that produces a very clear picture.

industrial design—the design of products that will be manufactured through mass production.

jetpack—a device worn on one's back that propels the wearer through the air using jets of gas or liquid.

mobile—capable of moving or being moved.

platformer—a video game in which the player-controlled character moves and jumps across platforms of varying heights while avoiding obstacles.

role-playing game (RPG)—a game in which the player decides the actions of a character within a detailed narrative. RPG players interact with other characters in the game to accomplish tasks or achieve goals.

sequel—a movie, game, or other work that continues the story of a previous work.

side-scroller—a video game in which the action is viewed from the side as the player-controlled character moves across the screen, usually from left to right.

spherical (SFIHR-i-kuhl)—having a globe-shaped body.

3-D—having length, width, and depth, or appearing to have these dimensions. *3-D* stands for "three-dimensional."

2-D—having length and width but lacking the appearance of depth. *2-D* stands for "two-dimensional."

ONLINE RESOURCES

Booklinks
NONFICTION NETWORK
FREE! ONLINE NONFICTION RESOURCES

To learn more about *Mario*, please visit **abdobooklinks.com** or scan this QR code. These links are routinely monitored and updated to provide the most current information available.

INDEX